FINISHING ON TIME

FINISHING ON TIME

Roadmap to Kingdom success

ESAU JASPER

XULON PRESS

Xulon Press
2301 Lucien Way #415
Maitland, FL 32751
407.339.4217
www.xulonpress.com

© 2018 by Esau Jasper

Edited by Xulon Press.

All rights reserved solely by the author. The author guarantees all contents are original and do not infringe upon the legal rights of any other person or work. No part of this book may be reproduced in any form without the permission of the author. The views expressed in this book are not necessarily those of the publisher.

Unless otherwise indicated, Scripture quotations taken from the King James Version (KJV) – *public domain*.

Printed in the United States of America.

ISBN-13: 978-1-54563-560-5

CONTENTS

INTRODUCTION..vii

Chapter 1   Created for a Purpose..........................1
  God's Plan
  The Path of the Just
  Service

Chapter 2   Discerning the Times......................... 13
  Alertness
  Wisdom
  Study for the Task
  The Holy Spirit, a Reliable Partner

Chapter 3   Preparing for the mission 29
  Impartation
  Acting on the Word

Chapter 4   Numbering Our Days 37
  Redeeming the Time
  Opposition
  Open Doors

Chapter 5   Accelerating the Mission 45
  Delay Factor
  Global Factor
  Speed Factor
  Creating Opportunities
  Divine Means
  Running for a Prize
  Being Different

Chapter 6	Mind-Set	61
	Keeping Focus	
	Maintaining Positive Confessions	
Chapter 7	Provision	67
	Human Effort	
	Divine Effort	
Chapter 8	Fighting a Good Fight	71
	Battle Against Sin	
	Escape Sin	
	Protection from Attack	
	Changing Strategies	
	Prevailing Prayer	
Chapter 9	Finishing Well	81
Chapter 10	Rewards	83
	Earthly Benefits	
	Final Reward	

INTRODUCTION

To every thing there is a season, and a time to every purpose under the heaven:

A time to be born, and a time to die; a time to plant, and a time to pluck up that which is planted;

A time to kill, and a time to heal; a time to break down, and a time to build up;

A time to weep, and a time to laugh; a time to mourn, and a time to dance;

A time to cast away stones, and a time to gather stones together; a time to embrace, and a time to refrain from embracing;

A time to get, and a time to lose; a time to keep, and a time to cast away;

A time to rend, and a time to sew; a time to keep silence, and a time to speak;

A time to love, and a time to hate; a time of war, and a time of peace. (Ecclesiasts 3:1-8)

Then we which are alive and remain shall be caught up together with them in the clouds, to meet the Lord in the air: and so shall we ever be with the Lord. (1 Thessalonians 4:17)

Wow! This is so amazing. We humans will not just suffer the dreadful experience of death, but we will enjoy the awesomeness of a glorious resurrection. The preacher Solomon appropriately provided some major contrasting views of life events that we will all experience on our earthly journeys.

From the Scripture passages listed above, we can easily arrive at the conclusion that there are two great events in the lives of mankind: birth and death. We entered this world through the threshold of birth, displaying much diversity in appearance, ability, and life circumstances. Nevertheless, we will all depart this world through the process of death, if Jesus tarries.

Most importantly, between those two extreme events are many other events of sadness and joy, hardship and ease, trouble and peace, failure and success, work and rest. The negative aspects are challenges that we must conquer in order to fulfill our divine destinies.

The exemption from death mentioned in 1 Thessalonians 4 is for those who are alive when Jesus returns for the church. As Christians, we eagerly await the inevitable return of our Lord and King. Kindly take a few moments and ask yourself these questions: What can you do with the remaining time of your life? Can you recover the wasted times and chances of your life? How can you make your life relevant to the kingdom of God in this generation? I am very optimistic that the answer to these

questions will become clearer as you dig into the treasures of His marvelous words.

And as it is appointed unto men once to die, but after this the judgment: (Hebrews 9:27)

I grew up being very frightened of the dark and the dead. I knew then that this was a result of losing both of my parents at a very tender age. By the grace of God, I eventually outgrew such tormenting fear. Yet looking back at that time, I realize that the real tormenter was not the darkness or the dead, but rather the uncertainty of what came after death. This fear of being lost and empty, as well as the uncertainty of what was coming, ultimately drove me onto a path of love, peace, and joy in the Holy Ghost.

And fear not them which kill the body, but are not able to kill the soul: but rather fear him which is able to destroy both soul and body in hell. (Matthew 10:28)

More than ever before, there is a great urgency on the earth for the church to begin manifesting the true purpose of the kingdom. The world is waiting for the unstoppable rise of sons and daughters who are carriers of the fire and anointing of the Holy Ghost.

For the earnest expectation of the creature waiteth for the manifestation of the sons of God. (Romans 8:19)

The church is ablaze, and no devil from the pit of hell can quench the fire of the Holy Spirit. It is time to locate your place in the kingdom and determine the fulfillment of God's purpose in your life.

Have you ever asked yourself why you were created? Are you fulfilling the purpose of your creation? Many people, including some Christians, are only existing, while others have decided to truly live.

I would define mere existence to mean availability of a person without any godly purpose to live for. Furthermore, a person living without a drive toward God and the destiny that our heavenly Father has preordained for him or her is simply existing. An existing person can be counted in the land of the living but is not fulfilling what he or she was intended for. Don't just exist—live.

For to be carnally minded is death; but to be spiritually minded is life and peace. Because the carnal mind is enmity against God: for it is not subject to the law of God, neither indeed can be. (Romans 8:6–7)

I decree and declare that as you read this book, the life of God will impact and overshadow you in an unusual way.

With long life will I satisfy him, and shew him my salvation. (Psalms 91:16)

It is worth mentioning that our heavenly Father has promised us long life. Long life must not be viewed as eternity on earth, but it must rather be perceived as God providing us ample time to fulfill our divine destinies on earth. As you read this book, I decree that the purpose of God concerning your life will never be aborted. You shall live long enough to fulfill your divine mandate. Everything standing between you and your destiny will be melted in the liquid fire of the Holy Ghost. Amen.

It is the glory of God to conceal a thing: but the honour of kings is to search out a matter. (Proverbs 25:2)

But ye are a chosen generation, a royal priesthood, an holy nation, a peculiar people; that ye should shew forth the praises of him who hath called you out of darkness into his marvelous light. (1 Peter 2:9)

Our heavenly Father is the King of Kings, and spiritually, His divine blood runs through our veins, as we are children of royalty. We are called to reign as kings and queens on the earth. It is truly an honor for us to unravel the mysteries of His kingdom. This makes a lot of sense when we realize that most of the precious substances of the earth, such as gold, diamond, jasper, natural gas, iron ore, etc., are hidden deep in the earth. Similarly, the mysteries of the kingdom are embedded within the mind of the Holy Spirit.

The Holy Spirit will take you through this book to uncover the myriad of spiritual truths contained within. You will discover or rediscover your purpose for existence and will accelerate with the realization that your journey on this earth could be over by tomorrow.

This is your time to affect your generation for God. This is the time to rewrite the history of your faith in God. Submit to the

awesome power of the Holy Ghost, and He will catapult you into a new dimension of service, grace, vision, and power. In Jesus' name, I pray. Amen.

1

CREATED FOR A PURPOSE

(Purpose Is the Reason We Exist)

To everything there is a season, and a time to every purpose under the heaven: (Ecclesiastes 3:1)

When a person buys an umbrella, it is easy to determine the purpose. The reasonable purpose for buying an umbrella is not to prepare for the winter, but rather to prepare for the rain. The purpose of a plane is not to travel under water, but to fly in the sky.

Our heavenly Father created everything for a peculiar purpose and a season designed to suit that purpose. Purpose is God's master plan for your life. It is the reason you were designed so uniquely. It is the reason for your very existence.

GOD'S PLAN

Before I formed thee in the belly I knew thee; and before thou camest forth out of the womb I sanctified thee, and I ordained thee a prophet unto the nations. Then said I, Ah, Lord God! Behold, I cannot speak: for I am a child. (Jeremiah 1:5–6)

We live in a purposeful world. Everything, whether good or bad, was originated for a reason. When God created light, it was for expelling darkness during the day. When He created woman, it was for help, companionship, and multiplication.

Wow! It's fascinating. Here we see the omniscience of God being displayed; that is, His ability to know all things. How could He possibly not know, since He is our Creator and the orchestrater of our uncommon destinies? We were conceived in the mind of God *before* our human conception. While we were hidden in the wombs of our mothers, we were known to Him alone.

Jeremiah might have been shocked to realize that God had such a high purpose for him, and he may have thought that his personality did not fit the demands of the office. He might have had other plans on his mind that he considered good for himself. Jeremiah thus said unto the Lord, "Behold, I cannot speak: for I am only a child."

And Moses said unto the LORD, O my Lord, I am not eloquent, neither heretofore, nor since thou hast spoken unto thy servant: but I am slow of speech, and of a slow tongue. (Exodus 4:10)

We see a repeated pattern here in Scripture, with Moses making a similar excuse to God.

Many people's destinies are terminated because of excuses, doubts, wrong confessions, and an unwillingness to say yes to the Lord. They offer excuses as to why they can't serve God. Some may say, "I work every day, including Sunday," or "When I'm done with my project, then I will start." They make one excuse after another, but time wasted is never regained.

We, as humans, have inherited the nature of purpose from our heavenly Father. It goes deep into our spiritual DNA. For example, God created the land to inhabit man and beast, but man invented cars for transport and houses for dwelling. God created plants for food production, but man invented recipes for taste and nourishment. God created humans to dwell on the earth and serve Him, but man created cloth for covering, medication for treatment, and the list goes on.

Our purpose might be either good or bad, based on the condition of our heart, but the concept originated from the Lord. We must always be driven by God's divine purpose to give our lives the spiritual relevance that He desires.

My spiritual background was in working with the religious committee at the campus where I grew up, but at that time, I was not saved. I was charged with the responsibility of running a Christian organization even though I was not saved. It was one of those activities we did as youth to prepare us for life in a challenging world. If you are in a similar situation, then get saved and get it right.

Later in my life, it was difficult to get me to go to church because of my fear that I would have to leave too many pleasurable things behind. When I did go to church, I was so uncomfortable trying to fight against the conviction of the Holy Spirit that was overwhelming. It wasn't until later that I discovered there is no ecstasy or delight greater than the joy that comes from experiencing the glory of Yahweh. Like many of you, I had my personal plans, but God's plan is always best.

For I know the thoughts that I think toward you, saith the LORD, thoughts of peace, and not of evil, to give you an expected end. (Jeremiah 29:11)

For my thoughts are not your thoughts, neither are your ways my ways, saith the LORD. For as the heavens are higher than earth, so are my ways higher than your ways, and my thoughts than your thoughts. (Isaiah 55:8–9)

God has a plan for all His creation, and we are integral parts. Our human tendency is to think that we know what is best for us, or we think we have answers to the many challenges we encounter. A plan birthed out of a carnal mind, however, fails or succeeds only to the benefit of the flesh, but that which is from above is above all (John 3:31). The building can't be greater than the builder, the servant can't be greater than his master, and the thoughts of man can't be measured against the thoughts of God.

Because the foolishness of God is wiser than men; and the weakness of God is stronger than men. (1 Corinthians 1:25)

Our Lord Jesus Christ is no longer embedded in flesh and blood as we are. He has ascended to heaven in a glorious body. Our natural world was created to relate to natural things. We humans can't see or feel spiritual things without divine ability. This is why God wants to use us, His children, as His point of contact to a dying world. Therefore, we must speak as oracles of God (1 Peter 4:11), and our hands must be perceived as an extension of Christ's hands. We were created for signs and wonders (Isaiah 8:18), because the Lord dwells in us by His Spirit.

Introduction

We might look small on the outside, but we can be a hundred-plus times bigger on the inside by His grace (1 John 4:4). We are the generation of greater works. We were created to do more than we expect; therefore, let us go out and surprise the world with the grace and power that have been bestowed upon us by our King. Our Lord Jesus Christ declared prophetically to this generation, saying:

Verily, verily, I say unto you, He that believeth on me, the works that I do shall he do also; and greater works than these shall he do; because I go unto my Father. (John 14:12)

In these final days before the return of our Lord Jesus Christ, God is relying on us to convey the gospel and power of the kingdom. Set up the alarm, warning your friends, loved ones, and the world to prepare for the majestic arrival of the King of Kings and the Lord of Lords.

Now then we are ambassadors for Christ, as though God did beseech you by us: we pray you in Christ's stead, be ye reconciled to God. (2 Corinthians 5:20)

We are God's royal ambassadors to this planet, reconciling the world to Him. We are emissaries of His Highness, and our kingdom is divine and supreme. God's desire must always be our delight. The world can't see Jesus Christ, but it sees us. It is our purpose to represent Him in all things: at our place of work, at school, in the street, and to everyone we encounter. We must beam the glorious light of heaven as that lighthouse upon a hill that cannot be hidden.

You may not understand everything that God is doing in your life, but He is always right. You may be tempted by contrary desires to run away as Jonah did, but be aware of the fate of Jonah.

But Jonah rose up to flee unto Tarshish from the presence of the LORD, and went down to Joppa; and he found a ship going to Tarshish: so he paid the fare thereof, and went down into it, to go with them unto Tarshish from the presence of the LORD. (Jonah 1:3)

Always remember that life is never a success without the fulfillment of God's purpose, and outside His purpose are many hurdles of confusion, fear, and anguish.

I will praise thee; for I am fearfully and wonderfully made: Marvelous are thy works; and that my soul knoweth right well. (Psalms 139:14)

…For unto whomsoever much is given, of him shall be much required: and to whom men have committed much, of him they ask the more. (Luke 12:48)

Cars are built differently and are suited for different situations. Similarly, all of us were made with different abilities and personalities because of our unique objectives. Nothing happens in the life of a believer for no reason. There is a reason for everything that is happening in your life.

If you are a talented singer, use your voice to glorify the Father. Every gift received from the Lord has an intended purpose. It is not good to bury your gifts and leave this world unfulfilled. Remember that to whom much is given, much will be required by the Lord.

For the invisible things of him from the creation of the world are clearly seen, being understood by the things that are made, even his eternal power and Godhead; so that they are without excuse: (Romans 1:20)

All that we need to complete our commission is already provided by God. He will not accept any excuse. It is time to put the kingdom first and accelerate the vision. We must walk by faith and not by sight (2 Corinthians 5:7). Let us press toward the mark of the high calling of God (Philippians 3:14). Let us work as if we were the only people working to advance God's kingdom.

For it is God which worketh in you both to will and to do of his good pleasure. (Philippians 2:13)

When we develop an ardent desire to please God, we experience a change in our expectations. Drives for unholy practices will gradually be quenched by the Holy Spirit, and we will begin to want only those things that please Him. Allow your purpose in God to become an obsession. If you have not yet encountered a word from the Lord, continue serving God wherever He has placed you. God is ready to give you a fresh start.

Brethren, when you feel that a task is too difficult, remember it is God working in you. When you stand to preach, remember it is God working in you. When you are to pray for that miracle, remember it is God working to do those things that please Him.

It is time to experience His wonderful purpose. It is time to allow Him to extinguish those destructive habits and replace them with a life of pious ambition. You must begin to see things with a heavenly perspective. God's purpose for you is becoming clearer and is inevitable. Your secret is faith, your Maker is God, your purpose is divine, and your reward is heaven. Amen.

And if the ear say, Because I am not the eye, I am not of the body; is it therefore not of the body? (1 Corinthians 12:16)

But now hath God set the members every one of them in the body, as it hath pleased him. (1 Corinthians 12:18)

Every part of the body is designed for a specific purpose. The eyes see, the mouth allows substances to enter, the stomach stores and processes food, the legs move us around, and the ears detect sound, but all these parts exist on one body. They might not look the same or have the same purpose, but they are equally important. When any part of the body is hurt, the entire body suffers.

Every truly born-again believer is a part of the body of Christ. It pleases God to place you in the area He has designed for you, and it doesn't matter what anybody else thinks. Do you feel jealous or discouraged because you don't have the eloquence or charisma of the next person? Do you feel insecure inviting such a person to your fellowship? You need to get out of the flesh. We are gifted with different abilities, but we all have the same Spirit, the same purpose, and the same Master. Our diversities are intended to complement each other for the perfecting of the body of Christ (Ephesians 4:11–12).

Introduction

THE PATH OF THE JUST

But the path of the just is as the shining light, that shineth more and more unto the perfect day. (Proverbs 4:18)

This verse speaks figuratively of the destiny and the character of every blood-washed and Holy Spirit–led believer. We are called out by God and set apart to take the path that was pre-ordained to give us a glorious journey to victory. We are those who have emerged out of darkness and a gloomy world of sin. We are expected to rise like an ascending sun above the horizon of life with increasing radiance.

And the child grew, and waxed strong in spirit, filled with wisdom: and the grace of God was upon him. (Luke 2:40)

The earthly life of our Lord Jesus Christ had many purposes for us as His followers, but one important purpose was to show us what is possible by faith. We are to emulate the processes of growth portrayed in the life of our Master.

Jesus Christ, who was in the beginning, according to John 1:1–3, limited himself in a human body and came under the law that He might redeem us from it (Galatians 4:4). He "grew and waxed strong in spirit," Luke 2:40 says. Our Savior increased spiritually and physically, even though John 3:34 declares that He had the Spirit without measure, as an exemplary demonstration of His interest in our complete growth. He wants us to develop and be firm in our Christian character, to maintain focus and steadfastness on the path ahead, and to increase in the accuracy and efficiency of our gifts.

Enter ye in at the strait gate: for wide is the gate, and broad is the way, that leadeth to destruction, and many there be which go in thereat: Because strait is the gate, and narrow is the way, which leadeth unto life, and few there be that find it. (Matthew 7:13–14)

Many people around the world are seeking to find God in the wrong places, but Jesus Christ is the way. Whosoever walks into Christ will certainly walk out of confusion and despair. He is the way to righteousness and the source of kingdom exploits.

The above scripture lays out two extremely different spiritual paths, which are manifested by the choices we make or refuse to make in this physical world. The wide gate is the most convenient path; many people are on that path, which leads to destruction, but few are on the narrow path.

Why did Jesus call these paths the "wide" gate and the "narrow" gate? In my opinion, He called one the wide gate to reflect its convenient accessibility to people. I think the narrow gate is so called because of its requirement of faith and discipline. Since the fall of our ancestors in the Garden of Eden, humans have naturally gravitated toward sin and disobedience, the wide way, but I want to focus on the narrow way.

The narrow way is not the most popular choice, but it is the best choice. Many people, however, perceive the sacrifice of holiness, obedience, and perseverance as an uncomfortable task and the last option in life, if they consider it an option at all. Nonetheless, those on the narrow path are not moved by sight, but by faith. Their obedience to God is not predicated upon an incident or accident, but it's based on an unflinching faith in

God. The narrow path leads to a delightful radiance of a glorious celestial kingdom.

SERVICE

But he that is the greatest among you shall be your servant. (Matthew 23:11)

Service in the kingdom of God is the engine that moves the plans of God into action. It brings progression, growth, and accomplishment to the body of Christ. It gives joy and fulfillment to believers, and it is the hallmark of greatness. The greatest among us is not the most honored, but rather the one who is the best servant. Service to others will increase the scope of our relevance. We need to serve with the abilities God has given us.

For it is God which worketh in you both to will and to do of his good pleasure. (Philippians 2:13)

Those who yield themselves to the full desire of God will easily discover the wonderful purpose of God concerning their destinies. Doing the will of God doesn't have to be a confusing journey, but rather, it should be a direct process resulting from complete submission to the Holy Spirit.

Submission to the Holy Spirit will put us on the glorious path of righteousness. He wants to work in us, quenching every evil fire in our lives. The Spirit of God will allow confusion to be overridden by precision, fear to be replaced by faith, weakness to be conquered by strength, and sin to be dominated by piety.

For sin shall not have dominion over you: for ye are not under law, but under grace. (Roman 6:14)

And we know that all things work together for good to them that love God, to them who are the called according to his purpose. (Roman 8:28)

The purpose of God for our lives must be embraced as the primary reason for our existence. Many times, it might not be what we expect. In fact, we might not agree with it, or we might even consider it a mistake. His ways might be different from ours, but it is only by doing His will that we can find true fulfillment.

For my thoughts are not your thoughts, neither are your ways my ways, saith the Lord. For as the heavens are higher than the earth, so are my ways higher than your ways, and my thoughts than your thoughts. (Isaiah 55:8–9)

2
DISCERNING THE TIMES

(Only the Holy Spirit Can Navigate You to Success)

And of the children of Issachar, which were men that had understanding of the times, to know what Israel ought to do; the heads of them were two hundred; and all their brethren were at their commandment. (1 Chronicles 12:32)

For to one is given by the Spirit the word of wisdom; to another the word of knowledge by the same Spirit; (1 Corinthians 12:8)

That the God of our Lord Jesus Christ, the Father of glory, may give unto you the spirit of wisdom and revelation in the knowledge of him: (Galatians 6:8)

There are many people who have acquired various kinds of knowledge, but there are only a few people with the sense to apply that knowledge. There are even fewer people with God's supernatural wisdom. It is impossible to be effective in the kingdom if you don't possess the wisdom to know what needs to be done in the time you are living. Spiritual discernment is

an unction of the Holy Spirit that enables you to function effectively as a commander in the army of God.

In the late nineties, I was visiting an iron factory community in Liberia. We were having a very lively but very unprofessional discussion, with everybody shouting above each other's voice to make a point. Suddenly I felt a sensational strike in my spirit, and I experienced an inner knowing. It was an awesome feeling with absolute certainty that God had spoken.

It was an unction from the Lord. I bent over immediately and realized that I needed to pray for a sister who was seriously ill. It was the manifestation of a combination of spiritual gifts called the word of wisdom and the word knowledge. I immediately obeyed His heavenly instruction and withdrew from the crowd to pray in the Spirit. I prayed in the Spirit until I sensed a peace that the burden was lifted.

The next day I traveled to Matadi Estate in Liberia to check on this individual. I met a brother along the route leading to the home of this person, and I asked about her. He said she had been very ill yesterday, but just as they were about to take her to the hospital, she became calm. I asked further as to what time this had happened. He recalled the time, and I rejoiced in the Spirit because that was just the time I had started praying.

ALERTNESS

For as many as are led by the Spirit of God, they are sons of God.
(Romans 8:14)

Christians need to be spiritually alert to the moves and instructions of God. We can't afford to close our eyes to what is happening around us. We are living in a world where wickedness is very alarming. The Spirit of God wants to guard, protect, and lead us, if only we will avail ourselves of His help.

The testimony presented above is intended to inform you that your heavenly Father really wants to be involved in your every moment. You can increase your spiritual awareness by committing yourself to the following:

Meditation

This book of the law shall not depart out of thy mouth; but thou shalt meditate therein day and night, that thou mayest observe to do according to all that is written therein: for then thou shalt make thy way prosperous, and then thou shalt have good success. (Joshua 1:8)

Meditating on the words of God will birth inspiration. Inspiration in turn will produce revelation, and when revelation is acted upon, it will release the anointing of God for prosperity, progression, enlightenment, and victory for the body of Christ.

Daily meditation of God's Word will give you a firm and unshakable foundation of faith in God and will also keep you in a place of blessing (Psalm 1:2–3). Keep connected to the throne by daily meditation.

Prayer

Pray without ceasing. (1 Thessalonians 5:17)

Call unto me, and I will answer thee, and shew thee great and mighty things, which thou knowest not. (Jeremiah 33:3)

Prayer is a powerful spiritual weapon in destroying demonic fortresses and strongholds, and it is also a medium of communion with God. Our heavenly Father is anxious to reveal nuggets of spiritual truth that will lead you on the right spiritual trajectory. May the giant in you be released by prayer.

Fasting

My knees are weak through fasting; and my flesh faileth of fasting. (Psalms 109:24)

But I keep under my body, and bring it into subjection: lest that by any means, when I have preached to others, I myself should be a castaway. (1 Corinthians 9:27)

We deny ourselves food and sometimes liquid when we embark on the spiritual discipline of fasting. Fasting keeps us more alert to the Spirit of God and enhances our spiritual fortitude. Nevertheless, it is not enough to embark on a momentary fast; rather, we must strive to live a fasted life. It is not enough just to abstain from food, but we must abstain from every appearance of evil.

Faith

Behold, his soul which is lifted up is not upright in him: but the just shall live by his faith. (Habakkuk 2:4)

Faith is our divine currency and can be used to provide everything needed to make us successful. It makes what seems

impossible, possible. It turns vision into mission, and it brings accomplishment that amazes the world.

Faith is not something we do, but something we have. The faith in us is measured by what it produces. It is impossible to please God without faith (Hebrews 11:6). We must believe that God is a promise keeper.

The world may see you as a nobody, but God sees you as somebody. The world may say it is impossible, but you can say it is possible by faith. "If thou canst believe, all things are possible to him that believeth" (Mark 9:23 KJV).

Obedience

If ye be willing and obedient, ye shall eat the good of the land: (Isaiah 1:19)

Obedience is a critical virtue in determining whose servants we are. Obeying God is declaring to the world that He is your master, and obeying the devil means he is your lord. Continual obedience to God's words will guarantee us His favor and blessing.

Whenever we say no to God's directions, we are saying yes to the devil; and whenever we say no to the devil, we are saying yes to God. The wisest decision in every situation is the one that pleases Gods. Obey God always and deprive the devil of any bragging privileges.

WISDOM

Through wisdom is an house builded; and by understanding it is established. (Proverbs 24:3)

Relying on the wisdom of God takes away stress and bring freedom. It takes away problems and brings divine solutions. It takes away sweat and brings smiles. The wisdom of God places divinity over humanity. It turns failure into success, poverty into prosperity, regret into gratitude.

Human wisdom may be viewed as the proper application of knowledge acquired or a judgment based on sound reasoning. Divine wisdom, however, goes beyond such a definition because we act, not based on what we feel or think, but what the mind of God says concerning our situation.

Howbeit we speak wisdom among them that are perfect: yet not the wisdom of this world, nor of the princes of this world, that come to nought. (1 Corinthians 2:6)

Run Wisely

I therefore so run, not as uncertainly; so fight I, not as one that beateth the air. (1 Corinthians 9: 26)

If the iron be blunt, and he do not whet the edge, then must he put to more strength: but wisdom is profitable to direct. (Ecclesiastes 10:10)

These verses are so profound. They clearly reveal that life can be very difficult, and the simple things can become complex in the absence of wisdom. The wisdom of God, however, makes success certain and eliminates unnecessary delays.

You cannot expect to make a timely finish to a divine assignment by running with uncertainty or beating the air aimlessly. The wisdom of God will stir you in the direction of victory and make the job easier.

In the book of 1 Kings, we see a brilliant display of supernatural wisdom. In this portion of Scripture, Solomon rendered a wise judgment concerning two ladies who were arguing over a baby who had died and one who lived. Both women asserted claim to the single living child. The king pronounced a wise judgment, based on the genuine love of the true mother and the selfishness of the one who had lied. This is a classic example of how a complex situation can be made simple by the wisdom of God.

Then said the king, The one saith, This is my son that liveth, and thy son is dead: and the other saith, Nay; but thy son is the dead, and my son is the living.

And the king said, Bring me a sword. And they brought a sword before the king.

And the king said, Divide the living child in two, and give half to the one, and half to the other.

Then spake the woman whose the living child was unto the king, for her bowel yearned upon her son, and she said, O my lord, give her the living child, and in no wise slay it. But the other said, Let it be neither mine nor thine, but divide it.

Then the king answered and said, Give her the living child, and in no wise slay it: she is the mother thereof. (1 Kings 3:23–27)

The Spirit of the Lord is the spirit of wisdom and understanding, the spirit of counsel and might, the spirit of knowledge and the fear of the Lord. The Spirit is the distributor of wisdom, but we are required to ask for it.

And the spirit of the LORD shall rest upon him, the spirit of wisdom and understanding, the spirit of counsel and might, the spirit of knowledge and of the fear of the LORD; (Isaiah 11:2)

If any of you lack wisdom, let him ask of God, that giveth to all men liberally, and upbraideth not; and it shall be given him. (James 1:5)

I will be quick to say that there may be times in your life when you do not understand why God is instructing you to do certain things. No matter what, always stay confident in Him. The Spirit of God and the Word of God must always be your guard.

Have you ever been faced with a situation where obeying the Father's voice was difficult? Does it seem like you know what to do but fear doing it? Are you being held by guilt and unbelieve? Did you take a decision towards God but experienced a trouble conscience because of your attachments? Let me remind you of the scripture that states:

For if our heart condemn us, God is greater than our heart, and knoweth all things. (1 John 3:20)

Wisdom is the pathway to the fulfillment of destiny, understanding keeps us firm amidst contradictions, and faith enables us to withstand the challenges along the way.

If the iron be blunt, and he do not whet the edge, then must he put to more strength: but wisdom is profitable to direct. (Ecclesiastes 10:10)

Discerning The Times

*The fear of the L*ORD *is the beginning of wisdom…* (Psalms 111:10)

For God hath not given us the spirit of fear; but of power, and of love, and of a sound mind. (2 Timothy 1:7)

The above scriptures truly confirm that wisdom is the divine pathway to success. As you run this race, the Holy Spirit will put up signs similar to the signs you see on any street. There are times He will tell you to stop, to avoid an accident, slow down, to exercise caution, and go, to continue accelerating. Other times He may take you on a detour to save you from a dangerous path. In short, the Holy Spirit will keep you safe from unnecessary perils.

There is a seeming contradiction concerning fear in the Scriptures. That's because there are actually two kinds of fear. There is fear that intimidates and endeavors to hinder our movement for God, but there is also another kind of fear that motivates and constrains us to move forward. The first is a tormenting fear, but the second speaks of the fear of the Lord.

Scripture declares the fear of the Lord as the genesis of wisdom. It is based on the respect, reverence, and awesomeness of God. Do you love God to the point that you are disappointed, hurt, or uncomfortable when doing something wrong? Does your troubled conscience bring you to a place where you ask yourself, how can I make it right? That is the fear of the Lord.

There was a time in Liberia when the government did not want people preaching in the street, but I was already scheduled for a street meeting. Police were arresting people and taking them to jail. This was the first time this had ever happened, and the reason given was that there were too many street preachers. I received this announcement just as I was preparing for my street meeting.

I felt a strong leading in my spirit to honor my commitment to preach. I mounted my public-address system and drums and began worshiping in the heart of the city. Admittedly, I was afraid for a moment that I might get arrested and put in jail. Nevertheless, that did not stop me.

When I began preaching, the police task force paused and began listening to the words of God. The anointing of God was so strong that the awesome fear of the Lord rested upon everyone, including the police. They later drove on and allowed the service to continue. Glory to God in the highest!

The fear of the Lord will give you the wisdom to make godly choices. Your utmost desire will be to please God rather than yourself. The sacrifices of holiness will no longer be a divergence, but a decision.

Wisdom and knowledge is granted unto thee; and I will give thee riches, and wealth, and honour, such as none of the kings have had that have been before thee, neither shall there any after thee have the like. (2 Chronicles 1:12)

God asked Solomon to make a request of Him without any limitations or restrictions. Imagine if He were to ask us today, what can I give you? Many requests would be made from self-aggrandizement or selfishness: Please, Lord, give me wealth, fame, power, or long life. Solomon, however, answered wisely by asking for wisdom to lead God's people.

King Solomon asked for wisdom, and God blessed him above measure with it. He also added riches, honor, and wealth. It is dangerous trying to succeed by chance. We must be sensitive to the timing of God.

STUDY FOR THE TASK

Study to shew thyself approved unto God, a workman that needeth not to be ashamed, rightly dividing the word of truth. (2 Timothy 2:15)

In the first year of his reign I Daniel understood by books …. (Daniel 9:2)

The sons of Issachar were commanders of their brethren because they had the wisdom of God to know what Israel needed to do in each situation and at a given time. Daniel understood the plans and timing of God by reading books.

During those days, the common custom of wise men was to study the world around them. They took a great deal of time to study nature, momentous occurrences, times, revelations, and many other things. Through these careful studies, God allowed them to access information that was vital to what they needed to do as a people and a nation.

But the Comforter, which is the Holy Ghost, whom the Father will send in my name, he shall teach you all things, and bring all things to your remembrance, whatsoever I have said unto you. (John 14:26)

My people are destroyed because of lack of knowledge: because thou hast rejected knowledge, I will also reject thee, that thou shalt be no priest to me: seeing thou hast forgotten the law of thy God, I will also forget thy children. (Hosea 4:6)

Studying God's Word will distinguish us from others and make us wise. When a person is ill and goes for treatment, the doctor must know the right antidote to give. So it is with us as children of the King. We need the Word of God embedded in our souls before it can release life out of us. We need to be addicted to God's enacted words and allow the spirit of His words to permeate our souls, saturate our spirits, and be engrafted into our hearts.

Many people are limited in this present world because they have a limited intake of the Word of God. We need natural food for physical strength and nourishment, and in the same way, we need the Word of God to provide us with spiritual strength and nourishment. We cannot afford to operate outside the presence and provision of God because it is extremely risky and dangerous. The more time we spend before His throne studying and carrying on other spiritual exercises, the more the anointing will rub off on us and enable us to develop the mind of Christ; and the mind of Christ is a superior mind that launches us into a new realm of the supernatural.

I declare to you that the level and quality of information you receive will determine the level of inspiration you can impart, and higher inspiration will lead you to a greater reformation.

THE HOLY SPIRIT, A RELIABLE PARTNER

But the Comforter, which is the Holy Ghost, whom the Father will send in my name, he shall teach you all things, and bring all things to your remembrance, whatsoever I have said unto you. (John 14:26)

Since creation, God has manifested Himself to humanity in three unique ways. The patriarch and people of the Old Testament referred to God predominantly as the Father. Then, at the initiation of the New Testament, the dominant personality was God the Son (Jesus Christ). Now, in our time and age, the dominant personality upon the earth is the Holy Spirit.

Are you wondering how to find the path to a successful destiny? A global positioning system (GPS) may give you direction from one point to another, but only the Holy Spirit can navigate you to success.

Trust in the LORD with all thine heart; and lean not unto thine own understanding. In all thy ways acknowledge him, and he shall direct thy paths. (Proverbs 3:5–6)

Covenant with God to put Him first in all things. Always acknowledge God's will concerning your destiny, and He will grant you remarkable success. I would like to quickly inject that covenant must come before the commission, and your Master before the mission.

For what man knoweth the things of man, save the spirit of man which is in him? even so the things of God knoweth no man, but the Spirit of God. Now we have received, not the spirit of the world, but the spirit which is of God; that we might know the things that are freely given to us of God. (1 Corinthians 2:11–12)

One reason some nations are great and feared by smaller nations is because of their ability to see things by using satellites. This helps them to make informed decisions concerning specific challenges. Human satellites or technologies can focus on only one site at a time, but the Spirit of God is omniscient (all-knowing), omnipotent (all-powerful), and omnipresent (present everywhere). He is willing to lead us into our place of promise and enable us to access vital information that can turn us into true champions of faith.

Whither shall I go from thy Spirit? or whither shall I flee from thy presence? If I ascend up into heaven, thou art there: if I make my bed in hell, behold, thou art there. If I take wings of the morning, and dwell in the uttermost parts of the sea; even there shall thy hand lead me, and thy right hand shall hold me. (Psalms 139:7–10)

The Holy Spirit must not be just Lord and master of our lives, but He must also be our closest partner on this journey called destiny.

For as many as are led by the Spirit of God, they are the sons of God. (Romans 8:14)

Ladies and gentlemen, there is no need to wait for the Holy Spirit, since He is already on the earth with us. Since the arrival of the Holy Spirit on the day of Pentecost, He has not left us. He is with us and in us working wonders. I declare that after today, you will always be aware of His presence and begin to do what you have been ordained to do.

But ye shall receive power, after that the Holy Ghost is come upon you: and ye shall be witnesses unto me both in Jerusalem, and in all Judea, and Samaria, and unto the uttermost part of the earth. (Acts.1:8)

And there appeared unto them cloven tongues like as of fire, and it sat upon each of them. And they were all filled with the Holy Ghost, and began to speak with other tongues, as the Spirit gave them utterance. (Acts 2:3)

3
PREPARING FOR THE MISSION

(Preparation Propels Us)

Preparation is fundamental to propelling us into a glorious destiny. It makes us ready for the challenges that lie ahead. However, some of you may be asking, when does God start to prepare us? Is it before we are born again or after?

Then the word of the LORD came unto me, saying, Before I formed thee in the belly I knew thee; and before thou camest forth out of the womb I sanctified thee, and I ordained thee a prophet unto the nations. (Jeremiah 1:4–5)

God knew our destiny even before our conception. The psalmist David acknowledged the fact that he, and all of humanity, was fearfully and wonderfully made (Psalm 139:14). This points to the fact that our Creator took His precious time and wisdom to create us individually. He designed us with different abilities to enable us to fit into His purpose. Our distinction and ordination were settled before our birth. This makes it possible for us to be successful.

IMPARTATION

For I long to see you, that I may impart unto you some spiritual gift, to the end ye may be established. (Romans 1:11)

Neglect not the gift that is in thee, which was given thee by prophecy, with the laying on of hands of the presbytery. (1 Timothy 4:14)

We were alive in the infinite mind of God before our human conception. He is familiar with our natural and spiritual components because it was He who designed us. We exist on this earth to fulfill a destiny.

Impartation is the process by which God directly or indirectly bestows or communicates supernatural abilities or knowledge to us. We receive impartation by connecting to the Spirit of His Word or to an anointed woman or man of God. In John 6:63, Jesus said, "The words that I speak unto you, they are spirit and they are life." Our addiction to the Word of God will infuse more of the life and the Spirit of Yahweh into us. Let me be quick to mention that every good gift is from above, from the Father of light.

Meditation on the Word and the declaration upon our lives by anointed servants of God using the gift of prophecy or the laying on of hands will release a dynamic spiritual strength and ability called gifts. These gifts can also be imparted or cultivated by developing a personal and intimate relationship with the heavenly Father. The desire we have for God, coupled with the sacrifices we are willing to make in prayer, fasting, meditation, and obedience to His words, will increase the grace upon our lives.

Preparing For The Mission

Saul, the son of Kish, who was a Benjamite, decided to meet the prophet (seer) Samuel concerning his father's lost asses. During his time with the man of God, he received an immediate impartation. The Spirit of the Lord came upon Saul, and amazingly, he began to prophesy. The people were shocked at the sudden manifestation and asked, "Is Saul among the prophets?"

Your life can become a supernatural amazement as you sincerely walk with great men and women of God. Don't miss the opportunity to encounter grace from those servants of God who are sent across your path. Elijah imparted into the life of Elisha, Moses imparted into the life of Joshua, Paul imparted into the lives of Titus and Timothy, and the list goes on.

Then Samuel took a vial of oil, and poured it upon his head, and kissed him, and said, Is it not because the Lord hath anointed thee to be captain over his inheritance? (1 Samuel 10:1)

And when they came thither to the hill, behold, a company of prophets met him; and the Spirit of God came upon him, and he prophesied among them. And it came to pass, when all that knew him beforetime saw that, behold, he prophesied among the prophets, then the people said one to another, What is this that is come unto the son of Kish? Is Saul also among the prophets? (1 Samuel 10:10-11)

ACTING ON THE WORD

Be ye doers of the word, and not hearers only, deceiving your own selves. (James 1:22)

For as the body without the spirit is dead, so faith without work is dead also. (James 2:26)

As we subject our lives to sound spiritual authorities in the body of Christ and continue in fellowship with the Lord, He will position us to enjoy the experience of His grace and anointing. The awesome spiritual atmosphere that engulfs such people is powerful.

It is said that experience is the best teacher, and I would like to further add that experience is also the best way to build confidence. We draw strength from the fact that, what one person has done, other people can also do. Since we have the potential of God in us, I must add that what no person has done, other people can do.

Mentally recollecting my experience of learning to ride a bicycle, I clearly remember the difficulty I encountered in trying to sit on something with two wheels. I fell so many times that quitting seemed a reasonable option. Nevertheless, I encouraged myself and kept getting back on. After many failed attempts, the day came when I could finally sit on a moving bicycle all alone. That day, I was convinced that I could ride, and I woke the next day with much confidence.

What would have happened if I had decided that enough was enough and took quitting as my best option? You are right. I would have never learned to ride a bicycle and would have eventually missed out on all the benefits that come with it. That is exactly what happens to people who allow doubt and fear to hinder them from acting on God's words. If we faint not but

Preparing For The Mission

continue in faith, God will reward our faith and increase our confidence.

When we pray and get results, a special confidence develops for more prayer. What we have experienced is always a reminder of what is possible. When belief produces results, our confidence becomes unshakable. The principle of the kingdom demands that faith must produce action, and action will eventually produce desirable results. The key to accessing the treasures of the kingdom is faith.

For as the body without the spirit is dead, so faith without works is dead also. (James 2:26)

People believe in different things, but the object of our faith must always be in Yahweh. Do you sit on a chair if you know that the legs are broken? I don't think so. The reason is that the chair is not reliable. It is faulty. I submit to you that the most credible character in the universe is God, and every other ground is sinking sand.

Looking unto Jesus the author and the finisher of our faith . . . (Hebrews 12:2)

No matter how sincere you are, there are times when you will get it wrong. When that happens, be willing to accept correction. Don't be deterred; keep acting on the Word, and it will grow your faith. Faith comes by hearing, but it grows by acting on the Word of God. Your faith is measured by what you do.

Look around and you will see people with enormous abilities sitting around or doing the wrong things. God expects that, as we experience the power of regeneration, we move in the direction of our calling.

And the LORD said, My spirit shall not always strive with man, for that he also is flesh: yet his days shall be an hundred and twenty years. (Genesis 6:3)

But God commendeth his love toward us, in that, while we were yet sinners, Christ died for us. (Romans 5:8)

The word *strive* indicates that God is persistently going against resistance to bring us into His plans for our lives. These scriptures prove that God has always been involved in our lives, even when we were children of disobedience. His unflinching love and expectations for us could not allow Him to do anything other than bring us into contact with destiny.

I do appreciate my days of growing up at the SOS children's village in Liberia. The director appointed me chairman of the campus worship committee. I was not a born-again Christian at that time, but I was excited, probably because of the influence or just because it was something I enjoyed doing.

Nevertheless, I was charged with the responsibility of inviting preachers to come speak and working with a committee on developing rules or bylaws for the service. I invited the preachers and typed our program sheet for Sunday service. Later I realized that God was preparing me for a life in ministry.

During this chapter of my life, God allowed me to learn and gain insight about things that would later prove useful to me. There are experiences we go through that our heavenly Father uses to navigate us into a glamorous destiny. I'm convinced that

both the hardships and good times, failures and successes, and errors and corrections are instrumental in His skillful hands in preparing us for the journey ahead.

We do draw strength from our experiences, but we need to continue learning as we go along. We learn in part and progress in stages.

For we know in part, and prophesy in part. (1 Corinthians 13:9)

And we know that all things work together for good to them that love God, to them who are the called according to his purpose. (Romans 8:28)

4

NUMBERING OUR DAYS

(Oh, Lord, Too Much to Do in Such a Brief Time)

So teach us to number our days, that we may apply our hearts unto wisdom. (Psalms 90:12)

Numbering our days, in context with this verse of Scripture, suggests an approximate calculation of our remaining days on earth and is intended to produce a surmounting desire to reinforce our service to God.

It is easy to understand this scripture by reflecting on the story of a wise lady who was told that she had cancer. Every morning she would wake up counting how many days she had left before being caught up to glory. She arranged and rearranged her life with grave urgency. She did everything she could because this was the one time she had to get it right. This is the approach of urgency the church needs.

"Numbering our days is the process of soberly reflecting on the shortness and uncertainty of life. This sense of urgency will enable us to ignite a burning desire to move faster and work harder for our Father in heaven.

Many people live in denial of the fact that they are getting older by the day. Others ignore the fact of the uncertain, imminent, and inevitable transition because of death or the rapture. On the contrary, we need to live as if tomorrow were never promised to us, and today is the only day to labor for the Lord.

I must work the works of him that sent me, while it is day: the night cometh, when no man can work. (John 9:4)

The use of the word *day* in this scripture symbolically refers to being alive. While we are alive, we have immense opportunity to serve the Lord. This is our day of fulfillment.

Every day, when you wake up, you need to ask God in prayer, Lord, what would You have me do? There is always something you can do. Call someone, visit someone, pray for someone, show love to someone etc. There is always something to do. The more love you share, the more love you will experience from the Lord.

REDEEMING THE TIME

See then that ye walk circumspectly, not as fools, but as wise, redeeming the time, because the days are evil. (Ephesians 5:15–16)

During my early walk with God, I had a revelation from the Lord in which I saw myself standing at the threshold of a narrow, bushy path that led directly to the zenith, or the apex, of a mountain. Along each side of that path were vicious animals standing in line as though they were expecting to make me their prey and devour me.

Then I heard a deep-sounding voice saying, "You must leave from where you are and travel to the top of that mountain." Then He asked, "How are you going to do it?" and I immediately began to quote the above scripture: "I must walk circumspectly, redeeming the time, for the days are evil." He responded by saying, "You are wise."

Later I realized that this was not just a personal revelation, even though it was that. God was emphasizing the fact that we all need to walk with wisdom and speed for an excellent completion.

Those who number their days have access to the wisdom of God regarding the things that are most important for now and the time to come. Many of us have wasted days and years of our precious lives in disobedience to the heavenly lifestyle. We have chased after short-term pleasure and forgotten long-term joy. We are working hard to achieve things for self-gratification, but it is time to work harder for the kingdom.

Furthermore, redeeming the time means to make up for the dishonorable lifestyle we have lived and to recover our neglected destiny. If you start a race poorly or late and are left behind, you need to run faster than the person at the front. Refusing to run faster will cause you to stay behind permanently, unless the front runner's speed declines.

To redeem the time, you must consider both bad and good as motivation for a glorious future in Christ. Forgetting those

things that are behind means to lose interest in those activities that hinder you from being the person you were created to be and doing instead the things you were designed to do.

OPPOSITION

For a great door and effectual is opened unto me, and there are many adversaries. (1 Corinthians 16:9)

When Sanballat the Horonite, and Tobiah the servant, the Ammonite, heard of it, it grieved them exceedingly that there was come a man to seek the welfare of the children of Israel. (Nehemiah 2:10)

The prophet Nehemiah's encounter with Sanballat and Tobiah the Ammonite supports the concept that evil is always in opposition to goodness, as darkness is to light. God inspired Nehemiah to rebuild the ruined or dilapidated wall of Jerusalem, but the enemies of the vision were determined to make him fail.

Now it came to pass, when Sanballat, and Tobiah, and Geshem the Arabian, and the rest of our enemies, heard that I had builded the wall, and that there was no breach left therein; (though at that time I had not set the doors upon the gates;) That Sanballat and Geshem sent unto me, saying, Come, let us meet together in some one of the villages in the plain of Ono. But they thought to do me mischief. And I sent messengers unto them, saying, I am doing a great work, so that I cannot come down: why should the work cease, whilst I leave it, and come down to you? (Nehemiah 6:1–3)

In opposition to every light, there is darkness; to every good, there is an opposing evil; and to every advancement of the kingdom, there is an adversary. Paul said "many adversaries"

are standing in the way of fulfillment. Always remember, there is no success without struggle, no progress without pain, and no crown without a cross.

When Nehemiah's enemies realized that God's people were activating the fulfillment of their destiny, they became exceedingly grieved. Similarly, the devil and his cohorts become angry when we decide to please God. They are angry because we are advancing the kingdom.

Nehemiah's enemies tried to lure him from the wall, but he was too focused to act contrary to God's plan. They said, "Come down and let us meet," but Nehemiah replied, "I am doing a great work."

All the diabolical plans against Nehemiah failed, and the enemy's plans against us will not succeed either. Nothing we do for the kingdom of God is small. Every assignment is a magnificent work, and we need to pay great attention. Our perception of the task will determine our placement in God's plan.

Nehemiah knew that his position on top of the wall was far more glorious than anything below. He continued to speak, asking, "Why must the work cease while I come down to you?" If Nehemiah had gone down, the work would have ceased, and Nehemiah might have been destroyed.

Every fear is overcome by faith in the mighty name of Jesus Christ.

For they all made us afraid, saying, Their hands shall be weakened from the work, that it be not done. Now therefore, O God, strengthen my hands. (Nehemiah 6:9)

The work of Yahweh is truly the greatest job on the planet because everything else is vanity (Ecclesiastes 1:2). Our boss is our Creator, and our rewards are everlasting.

Nehemiah's enemies tried to entice him to come down from the wall. This is similar to Christians being pressured to descend from their heavenly position in Christ. The Scriptures say that we are seated together in heavenly places in Christ Jesus (Ephesians 2:6). We must never leave the privilege of His glorious realm for the low life of degradation and destruction offered by the devil.

"Why should I cease?" Nehemiah said. This reminds me of Paul's question to the church of Rome in Romans 8:25: "What shall separate me from the love of Christ?" There is no reason to cease from our divine assignment, because there is much to do and time is running out quickly. We are working within a time frame (Ecclesiastes 3:1). Don't allow anything or anybody to distract you from making a mark in the kingdom.

OPEN DOORS

For a great door and effectual is opened unto me, and there are many adversaries. (1 Corinthians 16:9)

I returned, and saw under the sun, that the race is not to the swift, nor the battle to the strong, neither yet bread to the wise, nor yet riches to men of understanding, nor yet favor to men of skill; but time and chance happeneth to them all. (Ecclesiastes 9:11)

The first scripture declares that the apostle Paul had an open door, which he described as "effectual," indicating surety or reliability. Now more than ever before, the world is opening up for the gospel. Bible schools and churches are being established in countries that rejected the gospel in times past. There are many mediums, such as the Internet, radio, and phone, that allow the gospel to travel to distant places.

There is a real open door before us, but there are also many enemies and obstacles. Sadly, there are people and organizations doing everything possible to hinder the spread of the good news. In some places, Christians are being burned, imprisoned, tortured, and killed, but great is their reward.

Blessed are ye, when men shall revile you, and persecute you, and shall say all manner of evil against you falsely, for my sake. Rejoice, and be exceeding glad: for great is your reward in heaven: for so persecuted they the prophets which were before you. (Matthew 5:11–12)

The preacher Solomon reaffirmed the wisdom I am echoing. If I may rephrase, an early start doesn't guarantee finishing first in a race. Strength doesn't guarantee victory in a battle, because there is always the possibility of being outsmarted by a superior strategy. For a person to earn a victory, wisdom must accompany the strength to implement, and skills must accompany works in order for that person to succeed.

It's important that we focus on these words and expressions: *open doors*, and *time and chance happen to all*. God will continue to provide opportunities for us to accomplish the things we were ordained to do. *Time* indicates that we will be alive when God is ready to use us, and *chance* reflects on the open doors and opportunities that will come, not just for a selected few, but for all. Keep doing what you do for the Lord, and get ready to walk through the doors that are about to open.

In every nation, many people complain of the lack of opportunity, but the truth is that they have not prepared themselves for the opportunities that are available. It is sad because without preparation there is no readiness, and without readiness there is no accomplishment.

We cannot divorce success from the ability to recognize and utilize the blessing of opportunity. Every available job is an opportunity for employment, and similarly, every lost soul provides an opportunity to increase the population of the kingdom of God. Whether physical or spiritual, every vacancy provides an opportunity to work.

Are you allowing God to make you relevant in His kingdom? Are you laboring honestly for the Lord? If your Master were to come today, would He say, well done, or depart from Me? You need to answer these questions with sincerity because your destiny depends on it.

5
ACCELERATING THE MISSION

(Forgetting the Past and Forging the Future)

These are the last days; therefore, we need to move as swiftly as possible into the divine plans of God. Whether we realize it or not, most of our precious lives have been stolen by the devil. Second Corinthians 4:4 reveals that the god of this world has blinded the minds of them who believe not. We have been maliciously manipulated to do demonic bidding for the devil and his cohorts.

Having said that, it is only wise that we speed up the process of restoration and exploits in Christ. To accelerate the vision or mission, there are several factors worth considering, but I would start with these three: the delay factor, the global factor, and the speed factor.

DELAY FACTOR

(There are eleven days' journey from Horeb by the way of mount Seir unto Kadesh-barnea.) And it came to pass in the fortieth year, in the eleventh month, on the first day of the month, that Moses spake unto the children of Israel, according unto all that the Lord had given him in commandment unto them. (Deuteronomy 1:2–3)

Wow! How did it happen? What caused the delay? A journey that should have taken eleven days was prolonged for forty years. Forty years was a great loss of time, considering the life span of most people. Many of them died in the wilderness, on their way to the Promised Land.

The children of Israel had experienced the mighty works of Yahweh, including the releasing of the nine plagues and the parting of the Red Sea. Yet the question remains: why couldn't they make the journey within the eleven days instead of taking forty years?

The Israelites were not overwhelmed by the might or strategies of their enemies, but rather by their own unwillingness to maintain faith in God. They complained and murmured against Moses and Aaron, in disrespect of the words of God.

And the children of Israel said unto them, Would to God we had died by the hand of the LORD in the land of Egypt, when we sat by the flesh pots, and when we did eat bread to the full; for ye have brought us forth into this wilderness, to kill this whole assembly with hunger. (Exodus 16:3)

Yea, they spake against God; they said, Can God furnish a table in the wilderness? (Psalms 78:19)

Unbelief is an ancient strategy used by the devil and his cohorts to lure God's people into a trap of failure, shame, and unfulfillment. The Israelites foolishly doubted God's ability to provide food in the wilderness, regardless of the many miracles they had seen Him perform on their behalf.

Brother James teaches us that a double-minded (unbelieving) man is unstable in all his ways, and that man should not think he will receive anything from the Lord (James 1:7–8). The greatest catastrophe of life is not death, but rather life without fulfillment. Doubt weakens our zeal and destroys our faith.

If thou faint in the day of adversity, thy strength is small. (Proverbs 24:10)

This earthly journey is hard for the flesh but pleasurable to the spirit. Remember the words of our Lord in Matthew 26:41: "The spirit indeed is willing, but the flesh is weak." Many temptations and attacks will come, but never allow them to slow you down or destroy your purpose. God will deliver you if you do not faint. Staying connected to the Lord will keep your strength high, for we are not permitted to faint.

Many are the afflictions of the righteous: but the LORD delivereth him out of them all. (Psalms 34:19)

This I say then, Walk in the Spirit, and ye shall not fulfil the lust of the flesh. (Galatians 5:16)

We cannot allow destiny to be hindered by the power of delay. It is difficult to run when a rope is pulling you back, therefore unshackle or detach yourselves from any impediment.

How long wilt thou sleep, O sluggard? When wilt thou arise out of thy sleep? Yet a little sleep, a little slumber, a little folding of the hands to sleep: so shall thy poverty come as one that travelleth, and thy want as an armed man. (Proverbs 6:9–11)

Sleep is a very essential part of our lives. While we are sleeping, our bodies undergo many vital processes. Many researchers have shown that sleep solidifies our memories, grows our muscles, repairs tissues, and rejuvenates us. Physically, there is a time to sleep, but there is also a time to awake.

There is a spiritual danger in oversleeping. Time is precious because once it is lost, it can't be regained. You may have repeated events and situations, but you can never repeat a time already spent. Don't allow sleep or sluggishness to rob you of meaningful time.

Someone once said, "The neglect of today is the regret of tomorrow." As profound as that sounds, I also believe that as long as there is life, there is hope and faith. Moving faster, according to divine plans, always works in recovering lost territory.

Spiritually, sleep symbolizes inactiveness, sluggishness, laziness, and deadness. Oversleeping is for those who have nothing to do, and it will bring failure. It is for the children of the night, but we are children of the day (1 Thessalonians 5:5).

Accelerating The Mission

You can't afford to close your spiritual eyes in sleep by being inactive or sluggish toward the ministry the Lord has given you. God can't fully use a person who is spiritually asleep or physically oversleeping, because such a person is unwilling and reluctant. God has no place for sluggishness in His kingdom.

Sleeping Christians find pleasure in idleness and live very dysfunctional lives. It is not possible to advance if you are not willing to do what it takes to move forward. You can't expect to harvest your field if you have done no planting.

But while the men slept, his enemy came and sowed tares among the wheat, and went his way. (Matthew 13:25)

In this parable, I want to emphasize the fact that the men slept and were not watchful. If they had been awake, they would have been aware of what the enemy was doing in their territory and had the chance to prevent it.

Sleep, laziness, or sluggishness has delayed and destroyed too many visions for far too long. Don't allow this to happen in your life. Arise and be a part of the supernatural awakening that is taking place. God is raising up troops of mighty Holy Ghost–filled and fire-blazing militants upon the earth. These believers are not asleep, but rather marching and conquering nations and continents in Jesus' name.

Behold, he that keepeth Israel shall neither slumber nor sleep. (Psalms 121:4)

God understands the importance of alertness, and it is not in His nature to sleep or slumber. He is very alert about everything happening in the universe. He remembers every detail,

including the number of hairs on our heads (Matthew 10:30). We need to emulate the alert nature of God by being watchful concerning our lives and aware of the danger that the enemy represents.

Therefore let us not sleep, as do others; but let us watch and be sober. (1 Thessalonians 5:6)

GLOBAL FACTOR

And we know that we are of God, and the whole world lieth in wickedness. (1 John 5:19)

Our world today faces many global challenges. Economic, political, social, environmental, and religious challenges abound. Immorality runs rampant, with self-esteem dropping to the lowest point imaginable.

The situations in our world today are truly alarming. Our wildlife is being ravaged, our land is diminishing by erosion, forests are being depleted at an alarming rate, and millions of people are living on less than two dollars a day. I have seen people in Africa go without food for days on end. Widespread diseases such as Ebola, Aids, Diabetes, and others are exacting a terrible toll. Thousands more people are dying from avoidable diseases.

The devil is busy in the world today. Many people crave answers to the diabolical activities that are destroying their lives. The bloodshed, poverty, demonism, and sickness may not stop today, but God can use us to make a difference. We may not be able to absolutely eliminate all these dire situations throughout the world, but we can help people live victorious lives.

Scripture declares that whosoever is born of God overcomes the world (1 John 5:4). Every child is born with the ability to effect positive change. You are an agent of profound change as you embark on your divine commission.

SPEED FACTOR

Wow! I'm so excited to reach this point. God wants us, the church, to depart from where we are and move forward.

They shall run like mighty men; they shall climb the wall like men of war; and they shall march every one on his ways, and they shall not break their ranks: neither shall one thrust another; they shall walk every one in his path: and when they fall upon the sword, they shall not be wounded. (Joel 2:7–8)

In the words of God, we read a vivid description of His expectation and demand concerning the last days' advancement of the kingdom. Christians need not spend their lives sitting or standing, but rather marching on to victory. We need to be firm and move as quickly as possible with the full gospel. May the zeal of God increase in the world today.

Wherefore seeing we also are compassed about with so great a cloud of witnesses, let us lay aside every weight, and the sin which doth so easily beset us, and let us run with patience the race that is set before us. (Hebrews 12:1)

I therefore so run, not as uncertainly; so fight I, not as one that beateth the air. (1 Corinthians 9:26)

The writer of Hebrews indicates that we must run this race with patience. We might not reach our goals or vision at the time we expect, but we must keep running, and we must run with purpose and focus.

The prophet Samuel, Habakkuk, and King David declared at various times that "he will make my feet as hinds' feet" (2 Samuel 22:34; Habakkuk 3:19; Psalm 18:33). They were saying that the most high God would give them legs as strong and fast as a sure-footed deer. Why would they need this? The answer is obvious: so they could possess the needed speed to work expeditiously in fulfilling the heavenly mandate and the strength to maintain firmness. I declare today that you are mentally sound, spiritually alert, and divinely empowered for your journey!

But by the grace of God I am what I am: and his grace which was bestowed upon me was not in vain; but I laboured more abundantly than they all: yet not I, but the grace of God which was with me. (1 Corinthians 15:10)

The apostle Paul exclaimed that he was the least of the apostles, reflecting his humanity. This statement also insinuates regret for his past lifestyle and refers to the fact that he was the last of the apostles. Unlike the other apostles, he became an apostle after the death and glorious resurrection of Yeshua (Jesus Christ). While some may consider this statement of Paul's as a form of bragging, let us be reminded that the Scriptures were given by inspiration from the Holy Spirit. God has a reason for every word written.

Most of the epistles were written by Paul. Paul was not just a learned man, but he was also a man gifted with strong revelation of the Word of God. In fact, the apostle Peter wrote of the difficulty that could be faced as a result of the depth of Paul's revelation that he received from the Lord. what is a mystery to the world, can be made known to us by the Holy Spirit.

As also in his epistles, speaking in them of these things; in which are some things hard to be understood, which they that are unlearned and unstable wrest, as they do also the other scriptures, unto their own destruction. (2 Peter 3:16)

The statement in 1 Corinthians 15 "I laboured more abundantly than they all" is an honest evaluation of Paul's works in comparison with the other apostles. Look at the Pauline epistles of the Bible and read of his sacrifices, achievements, and contributions to the body of Christ.

There is also a strong possibility that Paul is the writer of the book of Hebrews. He was an apostle to the Gentiles (Roman 15:16), called to minister to a people who had no regard for Yahweh (God). He stretched the gospel beyond familiar grounds. Let us emulate his example of faith and labor. As Paul affirmed, it doesn't matter when you start; you can always work harder to accomplish your mandate.

For the kingdom of heaven is like unto a man that is an householder, which went out early in the morning to hire labourers into his vineyard. And when he had agreed with the labourers for a penny a day, he sent them into his vineyard. And he went out about the third hour, and saw others standing idle in the marketplace, And said unto them; Go ye also into the vineyard, and whatsoever is right I will give you. And they went their way. Again he went out about the sixth and ninth hour, and did likewise. And about the eleventh hour he went out, and found others standing idle, and saith unto them, Why stand ye here all the day idle? They say unto him, Because no man hath hired us. He saith unto them, Go ye also into the vineyard; and whatsoever is right, that ye shall receive. So when the even was come, the lord of the vineyard saith unto his steward, Call the labourers, and give them their hire, beginning from the last unto the first. And when they came that were hired about the eleventh hour, they received every man a penny. (Matthew 20:1–9)

This passage of Scripture presents a classical illustration of God's desire regarding the urgency of time. The man in these verses could be considered an honest man, according to his statement: "Whatsoever is right, ye shall receive." When the work was done, those who began at the eleventh hour were paid first and received the same as those who had come early in the morning. Why was that?

I don't believe that the laborers were paid according to the time hired, but according to the work done. We can logically derive that those who came at the eleventh hour worked harder and faster to compete at the level of those who started early. You may be swift in starting early, but it is how well you finish that matters.

Whatever work is charged to your care by our God, do your best. Work hard, fast, and wisely, because the kingdom depends on you. Work as if you are the only person working. Work as if your life depended on it. Work as if it is the only task in your life.

Many people take pride in telling other people how long they have been Christians and how hard they have worked. You

might have been zealous and worked hard yesterday, but what about today? It is far better if we speak about improving in our work and walk with God. Starting strong is not good enough; we need to finish strong. Scripture states that the first shall be the last and the last shall be first. You don't have to be overtaken by anyone. Keep your zeal for the Lord intact. Remember the words of Solomon:

Whatsoever thy hand findeth to do, do it with all thy might; for there is no work, nor device, nor knowledge, nor wisdom, in the grave, whither thou goest. I returned, and saw under the sun, that the race is not to the swift, nor the battle to the strong, neither yet bread to the wise, nor yet riches to men of understanding, nor yet favour to men of skill; but time and chance happeneth to them all. (Ecclesiastes 9:10–11)

Though others may have a vision for a house, why don't you go for the towns, cities, nations, or the world, according to your grace? I am convinced that to underperform in the grace God has given you is taking the Lord's grace in vain. Move faster, stretch to fulfill your potential, and populate heaven and plunder hell.

CREATING OPPORTUNITIES

Whatsoever thy hand findeth to do, do it with thy might; for there is no work, nor device, nor knowledge, nor wisdom, in the grave, whither thou goest. (Ecclesiastes 9:10)

We must enthusiastically, energetically, and expeditiously move with industrious excitement toward the work of the kingdom.

We must trust God for the application of an indefatigable persistence to the fulfillment of the commission.

The phrase in the above scripture, "whatsoever thy hand findeth to do," is not limited to whatever is available, but also to things that are discovered by our effort to search or by openings created by His Spirit. When seeking opportunities from the Spirit of God, you will discover a surprising wealth of creativity that He has deposited in you. We see in Genesis 2:20 that Adam's divine insight did not disappoint him as he named all the animals according to the pleasure of Yahweh.

And he entered into one of the of ships, which was Simon's and prayed him that he would thrust out a little from the land. And he sat down, and taught the people out of the ship. (Luke 5:3)

Many people are caught in a web of limitation. They may be waiting for someone in their local church to leave so they will have an opportunity for ministry. Some people even go to the extent of plotting and undermining others just to have a chance to serve. Our Lord Jesus Christ did not need to dethrone the Pharisees, Sadducees, or scribes, even though He called them hypocrites. The kingdom of God is greater than any building or any group of people.

We read in the scripture above that Jesus mounted His pulpit upon a ship and taught the people concerning the kingdom of God. Furthermore, we read in Matthew 5:1–48 that He climbed a mountain to minister to the multitude that came to hear His teaching. The Lord has graced you with many great ideas and abilities regarding your calling, so use them to the glory of

God. It is always wise to win souls or develop disciples for the kingdom of God (Proverb 11:30).

I do believe that receiving the grace of God in vain is not limited to doing the wrong things but also includes refusing to do what we have been graced to do. I urge you to adequately utilize the grace that has been bestowed upon you.

DIVINE MEANS

And he commanded the chariot to stand still: and they went down both into the water, both Philip and the eunuch; and he baptized him. And when they were come up out of the water, the Spirit of the Lord caught away Philip, that the eunuch saw him no more: and he went on his way rejoicing. But Philip was found at Azotus: and passing through he preached in all the cities, till he came to Caesarea. (Acts 8:38–40)

Certainly, to every assignment there is a divine means. In the scripture above, the evangelist Philip exemplified the life of a servant on the move for the Most High. An angel of the Lord instructed Philip to travel along the road to encounter a perplexed eunuch. This eunuch needed help with the Scriptures and understanding salvation. Philip baptized the eunuch, and then Philip was suddenly translated by the Holy Spirit to preach to the people of Azotus. The desire of Philip to please the Lord resulted in an unprecedented move of the Holy Spirit to ensure success. God will dislodge obstacles, dethrone powers, eliminate foes, and then catapult you into your area of assignment.

Have you asked yourself why God didn't allow Philip to use a natural means of transportation? There may be other reasons, but the most striking reason, I believe, is urgency. The teleporting to Azotus enabled him to recover more quickly and speed up his trip. It shows the urgency to move faster with the fire and power of the gospel. There are people attached to your life who need salvation. Preach the Word with divine speed. I'm not saying that God will teleport you, but He will be involved in your every move for the kingdom.

Running for a Prize

Know ye not that they which run in a race run all, but one receiveth the prize? So run, that you may obtain. (1 Corinthians 9:24)

The apostle Paul encourages us to run that we may obtain the best prize. The good news, in contrast to what we are used to, is that the winner is not limited to a single person. This means that anybody can be a winner in the kingdom.

Lest I forget to caution you, it is not just how fast you run, but also how well. I know you don't want to be left behind on God's divine timeline. Arise and run. Move fast and wisely toward that goal that has been set for you. Focus your heart and mind on the commission, and your reward shall be great. Press against any obstacles until the vision is realized.

Brethren, I count not myself to have apprehended: but this one thing I do, forgetting those things which are behind, and reaching forth unto those things which are before, I press towards the mark for the prize of the high calling God in Christ Jesus. (Philippians 3:13–14)

BEING DIFFERENT

But my servant Caleb, because he had another spirit with him, and hath followed me fully, him will I bring into the land whereinto he went; and his seed shall possess it. (Numbers 14:24)

Apparently, God had a reason for not mentioning Joshua in this passage, since, in fact, it was both Joshua and Caleb who had brought pleasing reports to God.

Moses sent twelve men on an espionage mission, one from each tribe. Ten of these men returned with evil reports, contradicting a portion of what God had promised. Though the land flowed with milk, honey, and fruit, they nevertheless said, "There are giants in the land. We cannot fight them because they are stronger than us." Joshua and Caleb, however, had another report, one that pleased God. Caleb said, "Let us go up at once and possess the land."

Out of the twelve men, only two men were resolved to follow God all the way. In my opinion, this ratio reflects what we see in the church today. There are few people with that "different spirit" in Christendom, people who won't compromise God's words and leading because of personal gratification. I believe that we are the generation to change that ratio.

When you continue to do what most people are doing, you will get the results most people are getting. To get a different result, you must do things differently. To get the best result in the kingdom, you must strive to be the best. Some Christians have become relaxed or discouraged because they think they have done their best. However, I say to you that if your best is not good enough, you can always do better.

God always wants to bring us to the point where we can do more than we expect of ourselves. We need to trust God for that different spirit because that is the spirit of courage amidst despair, faith amidst fear, facts amidst falsehood, and light amidst darkness.

6
MIND-SET

(It Is Not Over Until It's Over)

I will praise thee; for I am fearfully and wonderfully made: marvellous are thy works; and that my soul knoweth right well. (Psalms 139:14)

My soul hath them still in remembrance, and is humble in me. (Lamentations 3:20)

So that my soul chooseth strangling, and death rather than my life. (Job 7:15)

Humans have a trifold nature, of which the soul is a major part. The body allows us to maintain a physical presence on the earth, the spirit links us to the spirit world, and the soul contains the mind, will, and emotions. Many scriptures prove the ability of the soul to know things or remember things, to make either good or bad choices, and to react with sadness or joy. The human mind functions within the soulish realm of the body, which is an abstract realm.

KEEPING FOCUS

Brethren, I count not myself to have apprehended: but this one thing I do, forgetting those things which are behind, and reaching forth unto those things which are before, I press toward the mark for the prize of the high calling of God in Christ Jesus. (Philippians 3:13–14)

To fulfill our destinies, we must be overwhelmingly obsessed with vision. The primary strategy of the devil and his cohorts is to distract us from the task at hand, which is why he is known as the deceiver. Our ancestors, Adam and Eve, were the first victims of his deception, and they suffered terrible consequences. Therefore, we can't afford to take our focus off the path that the Lord has set for us. The systems of the world and the devices of the devil are intended to pull us into retrogression, but our eyes must be set on the prize of His high calling.

For as he thinketh in his heart, so is he: Eat and drink, saith he to thee; but his heart is not with thee. (Proverbs 23:7)

Most people are not who they profess to be, but they are the image of the obsession of their heart. The heart is the mind of the soul, and it contains the intellect, emotions, and will. The brain processes thoughts and filters concepts that are then sent into the heart. At that point, the thought begins to either discourage or motivate us. It becomes a desire and a determinant of who we are.

Our decisions in life make the difference between our failure or success. The condition of our heart is responsible for the

choices we make, so we must let the words of God guide it, because God is greater than our heart (1 John 3:20).

The real you is a reflection of what has occupied your mind or soul. When you think on the death of a loved one, your countenance will be sad. On the other hand, when you think of something exciting, you will be excited. Similarly, the thought of what God has done will increase your faith regarding what He is yet to do.

I know both how to be abased, and I know how to abound: every where and in all things I am instructed both to be full and to be hungry, both to abound and to suffer need. I can do all things through Christ which strengtheneth me. (Philippians 4:12–13)

In any competition, you are not rewarded because you started, but rather because you ended what you started. In this journey of life, we need to maintain focus and consistency until the end.

Paul informs us, from the wealth of his experience of walking with God, that there may be times when we are uncomfortable. We may not have what is naturally needed in order to succeed, but God is abundantly more than enough for any need we might have. There may be times when God allows us to leave the place of plenty and go into the place of lack. What will you do if that time should come?

In times of lack, we must trust God and continue forward, whether it seems possible or not. We may run out of supplies, but we must not run out of faith or courage. As long as there is faith, ultimately there will be success.

During my first visit to the Federal Republic of Nigeria, I took along a brother who was a citizen of Nigeria. He and a friend had traveled to Liberia without knowing anybody. I came across these men and made them my responsibility. One was named Charles, and the other was Frank. Charles had left Liberia earlier, so I decided to travel with Frank to his home. This was during the early days of my ministry.

I used the money for the trip to cover our transportation costs and food, with the hope that Frank would offer me accommodation. Upon our arrival, he said that his sister had died, and he had to travel to Imo State immediately. This was unexpected and a great inconvenience.

I had no more money, but I didn't give up on God. God provided me with food and a place to sleep in a strange land, even though I was completely out of money. Through this, I learned the secret of abounding and being abased.

After sleeping for the night, I woke the next morning and prayed concerning my situation. I was on a mission of faith. I was directed to a church, and when I arrived there, I introduced myself. I met Pastor Olumide at Victoria Island in his church office. After we discussed ministry and the reason for my visit, a door immediately opened, and my mission was a success. Though I was in physical need, I trusted in the spiritual and the physical manifested.

Why art thou cast down, O my soul? and why art thou disquieted within me? Hope in God: for I shall yet praise him, who is the health of my countenance, and my God. (Psalms 43:5)

Mind-set

Are you discouraged? Are you thinking about quitting? Are you in a place of doubt concerning your journey? The psalmist has provided a strategy.

David was faced with an analogous situation when he spoke to the discouragement brooding within him. He confrontationally asked, with the desire to defeat negative emotion, "Why art thou cast down, O my soul?" and "Why art thou disquieted [uneasy] within me?" He continued by declaring who God was to him: "who is the health of my countenance." He reassured himself that the persona of confidence and joy was the radiance of God's grace.

Whenever you are faced with fear and discouragement, never hold back from confronting that negative emotion. Instead, recollect the memory of His greatness. Are you tired? Don't stop. Keep on going.

MAINTAINING POSITIVE CONFESSIONS

I call heaven and earth to record this day against you, that I have set before you life and death, blessing and cursing: therefore choose life, that both thou and thy seed may live: (Deuteronomy 30:19)

Confession with conviction will establish our possession. In the book of Genesis, God spoke creation into existence. We as believers must always pay great attention to what proceeds out of our mouths. We must use our tongues to establish our destinies in Christ.

Words can destroy nations and lives, but they can bring life and healing as well. The tongue might be a small member, but it is a very powerful member of the body, so use it to bring honor to the kingdom of God.

When words are released, they are enforced by spirits. No wonder our Lord Jesus Christ said in John 6:63, "The words that I speak unto you, they are spirit and they are life." Words release spirits into the atmosphere. An anointed word from an anointed heart will ignite a powerful, flaming presence of the Holy Spirit to destroy evil and revive, refine, and impact His people for greater manifestations.

Paul advises us in 1 Corinthians 15:33 against the harmful effect of evil communications. He declared, "Be not deceived: evil communications corrupt good manners." Your confession is the result of your conception. Your words are products of your mind. The strongest influence on our characters will come from the company that surrounds our lives.

7
PROVISION

(Provision Within the Vision)

And Abraham lifted up his eyes, and looked, and behold behind him a ram caught in a thicket by his horns: and Abraham went and took the ram, and offered him up for a burnt offering in the stead of his son. And Abraham called the name of that place Jehovah Jireh: as it is said to this day, In the mount of the Lord it shall be seen. (Genesis 22:13–14)

Humans are not the biological offspring of Yahweh, but we are His creations. Nevertheless, we have received His spirit of adoption that enables us to cry, "Abba, Father" (Romans 8:15). The immortal God is Father to His mortal creations.

A father is a provider, sustainer, and protector of his family, but God is greater because He is the source of all our provision. Our Lord Jesus taught us to pray, referring to God as our Father because He is our heavenly Father.

Abraham declared God as Jehovah Jireh because it is God who provides for all our needs. There are uncountable testimonies in

Scripture of times when Jehovah Jireh provided food, shelter, protection, maintenance, grace, or favor to His people.

Every good gift and every perfect gift is from above, and cometh down from the father of lights, with whom is no variableness, neither shadow of turning. (James 1:17)

Surely goodness and mercy shall follow me all the days of my life: and I will dwell in the house of the LORD for ever. (Psalms 23:6)

God is the provider of every good thing, and His provision never runs dry. He will not allow us to run out of supplies on this journey as we keep faith in Him.

I have been young, and now am old; yet have I not seen the righteous forsaken, nor his seed begging bread. (Psalms 37:25)

HUMAN EFFORT

A man's gift maketh room for him, and bringeth him before great men. (Proverbs 18:16)

The human aspect of provision deals with provision gained by using our God-given abilities. We are loaded with a diversity of gifts and abilities. The power of our gifts will announce us to the world. God will use the gifts He has given us to elevate us to a place of favor, provision, and distinction.

And Pharaoh said unto Joseph, See, I have set thee over all the land of Egypt. (Genesis 41:41)

From Joseph's youth, God blessed him with the gift of interpretation of dreams. The favor and destiny of this young man provoked envy in the hearts of his brethren. Though they were

planning to kill him, God provided an escape by allowing him to be sold as a slave. He was later placed in an Egyptian prison, where the manifestation of his gift eventually took him to the palace as second in command to Pharaoh.

We all have stories of how our gifts have connected and promoted us. I have seen talents raise people from the slums onto the stage of world elites. Work hard to develop your abilities because they will aid you in your journey of service in the kingdom. Religiously use what God has blessed you with to get to where He needs you to be.

God gave Moses a rod (Exodus 7:12), and Samson received divine strength (Judges 14:5–6). He has also provided something special for you. Discover it and use it.

DIVINE EFFORT

When thou passest through the waters, I will be with thee: and through the rivers, they shall not overflow thee: when thou walkest through the fire, thou shalt not be burned; neither shall the flame kindle upon thee. (Isaiah 43:2)

And the raven brought him bread and flesh in the morning, and bread and flesh in the evening; and he drank of the brook. (1 Kings 17:6)

The Bible is a catalog of God's supernatural provision. In 1 Kings 17:6–9, the prophet Elijah was instructed to move near the brook Cherith by the Jordan River, and God commanded the raven to supply him food in the morning and in the evening. When the brook dried up, God sent Elijah to the home of a widow to keep him fed.

In Daniel 6:19–22, Daniel said, "My God hath sent his angel and they shut the lions' mouths that they have not hurt me." God divinely protected Daniel. In Joshua 10:12–13, Joshua prayed, and the sun didn't go down until Israel had defeated the Amorites.

During the bloody civil war in Liberia, there were many times when I came close to death, but God supernaturally protected me. One time stray bullets were falling all around as I was picking greens from the swamp, and another time the Lord caused the bullets to get stuck in the door or the trees just to save me. But that is a story for another time.

The most striking example of God's supernatural protection was the time I had a pistol pointed to my nose by a ten-year-old rebel. As I stood with my suitcase on my head, he asked what tribe I was from. If I told him my tribe, he would most likely ask me to speak my dialect. Since I couldn't speak my native language, he would likely kill me, unless God intervened.

I simply said that I didn't have a tribe, and then he asked, "Where are you from?" I answered, "SOS" (the campus where I lived). He asked if I was an ex-soldier. At that moment, it was as if my spirit left me, and I had no fear of death. It was as though my hands and muscles moved involuntarily to push the gun away from my face. Then the Lord suddenly put laughter in the mouth of everybody except the two of us. Then I heard a voice say, "Small soldier, stop" (I think it was a military word that meant stop). I was grateful to God, but there was more ahead. From that experience, I learned that God will definitely see us through in Jesus' name.

8
FIGHTING A GOOD FIGHT

(Warriors of the Kingdom)

I have fought a good fight, I have finished my course. I have kept the faith. (2 Timothy 4:7)

The apostle Paul, like other great heroes of faith, received divine insight as to the completion of his earthly assignment. There was a completion only because there was a commission. His journey in Christ was challenging, but nevertheless, it was a good fight for the apostle regardless of what some may consider his late start. He might have started late in comparison to the other apostles, but he completed his mission on time.

In the verse above, I sense an undertone of militancy, athleticism, and spirituality, using the words *fight, course*, and *faith*. We are soldiers in the army of the Lord. God has destined a course for us to cover, and faith will see us through.

The apostle declared militantly, concerning the numerous challenges he battled against in his service to our King, "I have fought a good fight." Every Christian is faced with a daily

battle to remain firm in the faith, regardless of opposition. Society, tradition, and culture will determinedly pressure us to be conformed into the negative image of this world, but we must fight to stay firm, with no shaking. Evil forces are trying to influence and manipulate our lives, but we need to fight back. In this world, a war rages between good and evil, righteousness and unrighteousness, and light and darkness.

For we wrestle not against flesh and blood, but against principalities, against powers, against the rulers of the darkness of this world, against spiritual wickedness in high places. (Ephesians. 6:12)

Let it be known that our real enemies are spirit beings that are influencing people and nature to abort God's plan of redemption. These enemies of the kingdom are not invincible. They can be defeated, and the power to defeat them has been deposited in us through our new birth in Christ.

We are troubled on every side, yet not distressed; we are perplexed, but not in despair; persecuted, but not forsaken; cast down, but not destroyed; (2 Corinthians 4:8–9)

Regardless of the pressure exerted on us by our enemies, we must not give up our fight for the kingdom. Those who quit fighting are usually miserable victims of the vices of evil. They don't experience the joy of spiritual conquest and victory in Christ. You might have gotten knocked down in the mud of shame, disgrace, and self-pity, but God is not done with you yet. Rise up and take your rightful place on the frontline for the kingdom. It is not finished until it is finished. Quitters never win, and winners never quit.

If thou faint in the day of adversity, thy strength is small. (Proverbs 24:10)

Increase your strength by prayer, fasting, meditation, and obedience to the Word of God. Our Master and Savior taught us a dynamic secret when He was led into the wilderness for forty days and nights to be tempted by the devil.

And Jesus being full of the Holy Ghost returned from the Jordan, and was led by the Spirit into the wildness, Being forty days tempted of the devil. And in those days he did eat nothing: and when they were ended, he afterward hungered. (Luke 4:1–2)

The wilderness symbolizes isolation and discomfort to the flesh, but to the spirit, it is a place of spiritual renewal, empowerment, and conquest. We must allow the Holy Spirit to lead us into our own wilderness in order for God to empower us for the mission that lies ahead. Let us look closely at verses thirteen and fourteen of Luke.

And when the devil had ended all the temptation, he departed from him for a season. And Jesus returned in the power of the Spirit into Galilee: and there went out a fame of him through all the region round about. (Luke 4:13–14)

There is no birth without pain, no victory without a battle, and no testimony without testing. In the wilderness period of His life, our Lord rebuked the devil and all the negativity and spiritual contradictions that he represents. Jesus used Scripture to contradict and refute every contrary thought the devil threw at Him.

Submit yourselves therefore to God. Resist the devil, and he will flee from you. (James 4:7)

These things work hand in hand. We can't resist the enemy's attacks unless we are solely submitted to the authority of Christ, and we can't submit unless there is first a willingness to resist the appearance of evil.

Whosoever shall seek to save his life shall lose it; and whosoever shall lose his life shall preserve it. (Luke 17:33)

I encourage you to place your life on the frontline for God. Consider it a burnt offering unto God; then you shall be blessed with eternal life and great reward. Fight for the population of the kingdom.

Battle Against Sin

I believe that the greatest battle in human history is not the battle against nations, the fight against poverty, or the threat of nuclear war, but rather the battle against sin and the fight for human souls. I know this to be true because a temporary state of something is never as important as its eternal state. The battle against sin and unrighteousness is more spiritual than it is physical.

While we look not at the things which are seen, but at the things which are not seen: for the things which are seen are temporal; but the things which are not seen are eternal. (2 Corinthians 4:18)

For though we walk in the flesh, we do not war after the flesh: (For the weapons of our warfare are not carnal, but mighty through God to the pulling down of strong holds.) (2 Corinthians 10:3–4)

During the diabolical attack of the Ebola epidemic in West Africa, doctors dressed in a gear known as personal protective equipment (PPE). This equipment served as a shield against the virus, and anyone not properly dressed in this garb could easily become a victim of Ebola. Similarly, as long as we are submitted to the kingdom of God and walking in the spirit of His laws, we can't be overcome by sin. We must meticulously obey divine instructions to win the battle against sin.

But I keep under my body, and bring it into subjection: lest that by any means, when I have preached to others, I myself should be a castaway. (1 Corinthians 9:27)

The work of the kingdom is great, and we will need every ounce of strength in our bodies and spirits to succeed. Sin will slow us down or cause us to fail. It destroys our confidence and our relationship with the Father and can throw us to the ground in defeat. God forbid that we become victims of sin.

Wherefore seeing we also are compassed about with so great a cloud of witnesses, let us lay aside every weight, and the sin which doth so easily beset us, and let us run with patience the race that is set before us, (Hebrews 12:1)

Sin is defined in Scripture as "the transgression of the law" (1 John 3:4), but James simplified the definition of sin when he said, "Therefore to him that knoweth to do good, and doeth it not, to him it is sin" (James 4:17). We are surrounded by the

testimonies of great men and women who availed themselves to be of service to God. The records of saints should resonate in us and stir up a desire to emulate their courage, faith, and lives of purity.

For it is a fire that consumeth to destruction, and would root out all mine increase. (Job 31:12)

But your iniquities have separated between you and your God, and your sins have hid his face from you, that he will not hear. (Isaiah 59:2)

The declaration of Job continues to echo in my spirit that sin is "a fire that consumeth to destruction, and would root out all mine increase." It is so sad to realize the havoc that sin can cause us all. It was because of sin that Moses labored and did not enter the Promised Land (Numbers 20:12), Miriam was plagued with leprosy (Numbers 12:10), and the list goes on.

In my lifetime, I have seen churches and great Christian ministries collapse because of sin. I have seen the ruin of anointed men and the shameful disgracing of many sisters. Sin has defamed many prominent people, caused some elites to be eliminated, enslaved numerous sons and daughters, and resulted in many married people becoming single because of divorce.

Sin is a passion that is likened to a fire. If we permit it, it can overwhelm and consume us. Scripture asks an insightful question:

Can a man take fire in his bosom, and his clothes not get burned? (Proverbs 6:27)

Fighting A Good Fight

We can't take our chances with sin, if we want to finish well and on time.

Do you have a strong passion for something, even though it is biblically wrong? That is an evil fire. It is a vision killer, a Holy Ghost– quencher, a destroyer of purpose and zeal. It is intended to destroy many years of challenging work and benefits in store for you. It is a weight that will hinder your service to God. It is like a sleep that keeps you from working. May we always be determined to abstain from any appearance of evil and remain focused on the vision God has placed before us.

ESCAPE SIN

There hath no temptation taken you but such as is common to man: but God is faithful, who will not suffer you to be tempted above that ye are able; but will with the temptation also make a way to escape, that ye may be able to bear it. (1 Corinthians 10:13)

But his wife looked back from behind him, and she became a pillar of salt. (Genesis 19:26)

Our life in Christ does not exclude us from the fight to maintain righteousness and to walk in purity. There is nothing that pleases God more than a child who is walking in obedience to His words.

Hypothetically, if you were walking down a street and saw an open fence with the sign "Beware of bad dogs," what would your immediate reaction be? I don't know about you, but I would immediately assume that the bad dogs could be around anywhere. Then I would exercise caution and try to escape.

Just as we would try hard to avoid being bitten by bad dogs, even more must we try to escape being victimized by the dangerous venom of sin.

Flee also youthful lusts: but follow righteousness, faith, charity, peace, with them that call on the Lord out of a pure heart. (2 Timothy 2:22)

God has shown us the way forward. Let us not disobey the voice of the Lord, like Lot's wife did, and turn back. She suffered a terrible consequence by turning into a pillar of salt, but for us, turning back will destroy our increase and eventually destroy us. Let us flee even the appearance of sin.

PROTECTION FROM ATTACK

He that dwelleth in the secret place of the most High shall abide under the shadow of the Almighty. I will say of the Lord, He is my refuge and my fortress: my God; in him will I trust. Surely he shall deliver thee from the snare of the fowler, and from the noisome pestilence. He shall cover thee with his feathers, and under his wings shalt thou trust: his truth shall be thy shield and buckler. Thou shalt not be afraid for the terror by night; nor the arrow that flieth by day; nor for the pestilence that walketh in darkness; nor for the destruction that wasteth at noonday. A thousand shall fall at thy side, and ten thousand at thy right hand; but it shall not come nigh thee. Only with thine eyes shalt thou behold and see the reward of the wicked. (Psalms 91:1–8)

The task of working in the kingdom is a long and challenging period for all the faithful. There is no specific time as to how

Fighting A Good Fight

long He will have us serve before our departure to glory, but He will give us ample time to fulfill our destinies.

God has a protective coverage over our heads. We are protected by the spiritual canopy of His mighty feathers and within the reach of His shadow. Most insurance companies have a limit as to what they can offer, but God offers 100 percent coverage free of charge. As you work for God, know that you are protected because He is Jehovah Nissi (Exodus 17:15).

These promises of protection are the benefit of those Christians who remain in the secret place of God, those who maintain intimate fellowship with God and careful obedience to His will. We humans are weak and feeble, but God watches over us and doesn't sleep. Our God is a covenant-keeping God, and we are part of His covenant.

Behold, he that keepeth Israel shall neither slumber nor sleep. (Psalms 121:4)

CHANGING STRATEGIES

And when they could not come nigh unto him for the press, they uncovered the roof where he was: and when they had broken it up, they let down the bed wherein the sick of the palsy lay. (Mark 2:4)

Many generals are successful not just because of their superior weapons and technology, but also because of their ability to adopt different strategies. Changing strategies makes it difficult for the enemy to detect our moves.

The above scripture records that the crowd was huge and compact, but the friends of the paralyzed man had a mission to fulfill. They could have gotten discouraged and turned back, but they were determined and persistent in their desire to see their friend healed.

However, persistence alone was not enough to acquire success; they had to conceive a new strategy. Since it was impossible to gain access through the usual entrance, they decided to climb up on the roof and open it up. They did not consider the cost, because the vision was the most important thing to them.

To complete your task, you will need to conceive a strategy from the Lord. Don't argue—just obey.

Commit thy way unto the LORD; trust also in him; and he shall bring it to pass. (Psalms 37:5)

Whatever charge you have received of the Lord, you must commit it to Him for direction and success.

PREVAILING PRAYER

...The effectual fervent prayer of a righteous man availeth much. (James 5:16)

Prayer to our heavenly Father is the greatest advantage we have in this life of challenges. It will make us stronger than our enemies, and it will bring us wonderful results. We will be able to win every battle by prayer.

9
FINISHING WELL

(Well Done)

This chapter is intended to reinforce the fact that it is not enough just to finish on time, but we must also finish well. If our work is not properly done, we will lose our reward (1 Corinthians 3:13–15).

Behold, here I am: witness against me before the LORD, and before his anointed: whose ox have I taken? or whose ass have I taken? or whom have I defrauded? whom have I oppressed? or of whose hand have I received any bribe to blind mine eyes therewith? and I will restore it you. And they said, thou hast not defrauded us, nor oppressed us, neither hast thou taken ought of any man's hand. And he said unto them, The LORD is witness against you, and his anointed is witness this day, that ye have not found ought in my hand. And they answered, He is witness. (1 Samuel 12:3–5)

I am so challenged in my spirit regarding the character and stance of the prophet Samuel. God had been leading the nation Israel through a theocratic governance (God's rule), but the

people wanted to be like every other nation; therefore, He gave them a monarch, with King Saul as their first king.

Samuel delivered a farewell speech—not farewell from his office as prophet nor because of death, but from his leadership over the nation—and he asked God to be a witness. He asked the nation, "If I have defrauded, if I have taken what was not mine, if I have oppressed anybody, let him speak," but the people said, "You have done us no wrong, as God is our witness." Which of our national, religious, organizational, civil, or societal leaders could attest to such a circumspect life that they would sanction people to put their lives on trial, with the confidence of being vindicated?

I believe many men, women, and children today are serving God with integrity and uprightness. Nothing will make their service easier than having strong biblical character. In fact, the prophet Samuel was so pleasing to God that even his request for rain and thunder was not withheld from him.

10

REWARDS

(Our Labor Is Never in Vain)

But without faith it is impossible to please him: for he that cometh to God must believe that he is, and that he is the rewarder of them that diligently seek him. (Hebrews 11:6)

The two greatest sources of motivation or impetus in life are love and reward. Most of the time, it is not what a person already has that motivates him, but what he needs or wants. For example, many times we place toys before a baby who is learning to crawl because the baby is attracted to them. Because of that, the child is motivated to move toward the object. When a man is hungry, he is motivated to search for food. Motivation is strong when we are persuaded of a need or want.

I once worked for a company whose policy stated that a certain number of occurrences was tantamount to termination. There were times that I was running late, and while driving to work, I would be completely overtaken by anxiety. My focus then became firm, and my heart beat a little faster. I became a little impatient with cars ahead of me, and when I arrived at work, I would run as fast as possible to the time clock to scan my identification card. I wanted to keep receiving the reward of my labor, which was my paycheck. The thought of that check kept me committed and motivated on the job.

We do some things out of love and other things because of reward, but it is best to love what we do. When you are in love, the only thing that matters is pleasing the one you love. You will sacrifice without considering reward of any kind. However, what would happen if you were asked to work without compensation? The only ones willing to do that are those with great love for the job.

God is a rewarder. Those who are sincerely committed to seeking God will be rewarded graciously, but those who serve only for the reward will receive accordingly. Serve God because you love Him, not for any other reason.

EARTHLY BENEFITS

While we await the reward of our faithfulness, our heavenly Father has arranged it so that we receive the benefits of His blessings.

Blessed be the Lord, who daily loaded us with benefits, even the God of our salvation. Selah. (Psalms 68:19)

Our service to God is never in vain. The Lord is loading us daily with benefits—benefits that are packaged in many different forms. Look at the promises He made to Israel, of which we are also partakers:

And it shall come to pass, if thou shalt hearken diligently unto the voice of the LORD thy God, to observe and to do all his commandments which I command thee this day, that the LORD THY God will set thee on high above all the nations of the earth: and all these blessings shall come on thee, and overtake thee, if thou shalt hearken unto the voice of the LORD thy God. Blessed shalt thou be in the city, and blessed shalt thou be in the field. Blessed shall be the fruit of thy body, and the fruit of thy ground, and the fruit of thy cattle, the increase of thy kine, and the flocks of thy sheep. Blessed shall be thy basket and thy store. Blessed shalt thou be when thou comest in, and blessed shalt thou be when thou goest out. The LORD shall cause thine enemies that rise up against thee to be smitten before thy face: they shall come out against thee one way, and flee before thee seven ways. The LORD shall command the blessing upon thee in thy storehouses, and in all that thou settest thine hand unto; and he shall bless thee in the land which the LORD thy God giveth thee. The LORD shall establish thee an holy people unto himself, as he hath sworn unto thee, if thou shalt keep the commandments of the LORD thy God, and walk in his ways. And all people of the earth shall see that thou art called by the name of the LORD; and they shall be afraid of thee. (Deuteronomy 28:1–10)

These wonderful scriptures are a catalog of some of the awesome benefits the Lord has decreed upon the blessed. The Lord is providing both physical benefits and spiritual virtues for success.

FINAL REWARD

Every man's work shall be made manifest: for the day shall declare it, because it shall be revealed by fire; and the fire shall try every man's work of what sort it is. If any man's work abide which he hath built thereupon, he shall receive a reward. If any man's work shall be burned, he shall suffer loss: but he himself shall be saved; yet so as by fire. (1 Corinthians 3:13–15)

It is not just enough to finish on time, but it is also important that we finish well. If the work is not done properly, it is not done at all. Our work for the Lord will be tested as to what sort it is.

How are you building in the kingdom of our Father? Are you building a decent work, but with a wrong motive? Are you building with greed and deceit? Are you building for fame or popularity? Are you building for personal benefits? Earnestly reflect on the reason for your labor in the kingdom, and if you are guilty of any of the above, make the necessary adjustment. The kingdom of God is not about you or me, but about God.

Cast not away therefore your confidence, which hath great recompense of reward. (Hebrews 10:35)

You have come too far to turn back. Join all of God's militants as we march forward through the camp of the enemy, lifting the banner of Christ and gaining territory. You can't allow your confidence in God to be thwarted by the evil forces of doubt or skepticism. The reward of a victor awaits you.

For the Son of man shall come in the glory of his Father with his angels; and then he shall reward every man according to his works. (Matthew 16:27)

The next momentous event of Christendom is the rapture of the church. Those who will be caught up in the clouds will face

what is called the *bema* seat judgment, which some call the judgment of light. The bema seat is derived from the concept of the ancient Olympics, where the judge sat at the finish line and rewarded people according to their merits. Jesus Christ is our judge, and He will reward us accordingly. It is not a judgment of condemnation, but one of rewards.

Then we which are alive and remain shall be caught up together with them in the clouds, to meet the Lord in the air: and so shall we ever be with the Lord. (1 Thessalonians 4:17)

We must arise and challenge ourselves concerning the task that is set before us. We must be strategic and resolve to be the best that we are called to be. The battle may be great, but our reward is greater. When my days on this earth are ended, I want to be able to confidently exclaim with the words of Paul: "I have fought a good fight of faith." May He say to me—and to you—on that day, "Well done, good and faithful servant."

CPSIA information can be obtained
at www.ICGtesting.com
Printed in the USA
FFHW021422060919
54821336-60506FF